Letters to Jim

MEMOIR OF A 40-YEAR LOVE STORY

ESTRELLA ENGELHARDT

IBIS BOOKS

For my husband, Commander James H. Engelhardt,

and for all those who love and grieve.

Stories Take Flight at Ibis Books

The IBIS is sacred to Thoth, the Egyptian god of learning, inventor of writing, and scribe to the gods.

They are gregarious birds that live, travel, and breed in flocks.

And they are legendary for their courage.

ibis-books.com

PROLOGUE

On Thursday, June 2nd, 2022, USN Commander James H. Engelhardt of Sarasota, Florida, died in his sleep. He was 87.

He was born in Buffalo, New York, on January 10, 1935. He graduated from the University of Buffalo with a degree in Journalism.

Jim joined the Navy in 1956 and retired in 1983. He loved the Navy and had many exciting adventures in the South Pacific, Panama, Korea, Japan, South America, and more. He was Inspector General of South America, ran the logistics of the Panama Canal, and spent many years at sea in positions of command.

Jim had four children from his first marriage: James, Julie, Jon, and Jeffrey. He also adopted a South Korean child, Lisa, when she was six.

In 1981, he married his soulmate, Estrella, and was married forty wonderful years to her. For 37 of those years, they lived together in Sarasota.

Jim was a quiet man, tall, a little dark and handsome, and very well loved. His sense of humor was legendary, as was his kindness. His love and support of his wife Estrella was evident to all.

Jim's favorite place was Nellie's Deli, where he made many friends and loved to go five or six times a week for breakfast or lunch.

He loved to work with wood, to cook (he even wrote his own cook-book!), and he drove an Austin-Healey Sprite that he maintained for 53 years.

Jim is survived by his wife Estrella, his children, and also by Estrella's two children, Naomi and Marc, who loved him like a father, and his sister Elaine and her family.

We ache at the loss of this wonderful man and will miss him dearly.

1

Dear Jim,

This morning, for the first time in 40 years, I woke up, and you didn't.

How could you leave me? Now I have all this... space. All this time that I don't know what to do with.

Who will I talk to? When something happened, you were always the first person I told. Without you to tell, do those things even happen?

Life now feels like tissue. Thin and easily torn.

There's a bird singing outside the window.

I'm writing you because when I talk to the empty house I feel crazy. But somehow writing makes it feel like I'm actually talking to you.

This morning when I awoke, I pulled out the letter you wrote me all those years ago, the one I always keep in my wallet. I read it and cried. But I could hear your voice.

So maybe, even up there in Heaven where I can't see you, as I write you a letter, you can hear me, too.

Your Dearest Darling,

Estrella

2

My Dearest Jim,

This morning I took out your letter again and read it over and over. Who wouldn't fall in love with a man who writes so beautifully?

My heart aches for you. I can hardly see clearly enough to type this letter with the tears streaming down my face, but by golly I want the world to know the handsome and kind man G-d sent me.

Now I wonder... how can I love a G-d that took you from me? I feel ashamed to say that, but it's so unfair.

We must have said "I love you" to each other over twenty times a day in the last five years. It never got old or bothersome.

I need to tell you about your son, James Jr. We've been having a beautiful exchange of emails for over a month, while you were sick and through all the preparations, sometimes two or three times a day.

He tells me I'm his friend and apparently the only one he can talk to openly. Who knows why you two didn't communicate for years? I remember—was it 20 years ago?—that he came to our home for a couple of months and was drinking too much and that's when I said, "No, sorry, but I won't have two drinkers in our home," and you asked him to leave. Was that the last time? So much time lost. At least he listened to me and called you days before you died and told you he always loved you.

Tomorrow I go to see Shirley, my grief counselor. I have a lot to tell her.

I love you forever.

Your Dearest Darling,

Estrella

3

Darling Jim,

Today I was thinking about the crazy thing we did before we got married. I laugh very time I think about it, and laughter is what I need.

You picked me up at the train station, and we went to this very nice hotel in Panama. When we got there, we were both so nervous that you, instead of going to the check-in desk, went to the concierge. Finally, we went up to the room and started unpacking, but then they called up. They wanted our passports! *What?* We didn't need passports! We were residents of the Canal Zone, but we had to get out of there, because we couldn't risk being discovered, you know, conduct unbecoming an officer?!? We grabbed our gear and ran all the way down the back stairs, got into your car and laughed all the way home, nervous as hell.

That's why people usually go to "push buttons" in Latin America. They look like garages with a bedroom attached to it and there is a slot where you put some money into it and it's very discreet. No one sees you and you don't see anybody and you have a wonderful hour or two for just ten bucks. Also, if you want to order a drink or snack, there's a menu and a sliding window and again no one can see you. Pretty neat, right? *Why didn't we just do that?*

Oh to be young and stupid and running around Panama with you again, looking for a place to get frisky.

Your Dearest Darling,

Estrella

4

My Darling Jim,

Today was a screwy day! I had dinner at breakfast (*enchiladas verdes*) and breakfast at dinner (waffles), and some papaya and pistachio nuts as a snack in between. I washed the dishes and said the hell with it, I'm going to watch *Shtesil*, this Hassidic series on Netflix that has got me addicted. It's in Yiddish with English subtitles. Normally I don't watch something with subtitles, but this one got me. I must have watched for three hours, but now I'm happy to be here with you.

At one point today, I started to feel guilty about having a day like this. Fun. Delicious. *Normal.* How could I do that to you? But then I got a phone call from your youngest son, Jeffrey, and he said, "Don't feel guilty about this. You deserve a day that is simple."

My two children, Marc and Naomi, keep checking in on me. (How are they 52 and 60?? Time is unforgiving.) You and I never had children together, but I feel blessed to have yours love me the way they do.

Thank you.

Your Dearest Darling,

Estrella

5

DEAREST JIM,

I cry every day for you. I am crying now and I am in so much pain.
When I look through these letters on the computer, my heart cries out
to you. So many years. So many stories. I feel empty without you.

Even something as mundane as the list of your medications takes me
back to other times when I had to make sure you were taking the right
ones, since you could no longer read the tiny print on the bottles. I
would give you what you needed, and you seemed to be ok with that.
After all, you took care of me for over 40 years, and it was my honor
and privilege to take care of you.

I remember before we were married, living in Panama, I had to have
this miserable hemorrhoid operation and you wanted to take care of
me, so I stayed with you in your lovely little apartment overlooking
the Panama Canal. We sat and watched the ships go through. It was
a million dollar sight. But then I had to relieve myself in your bath-

tub—that was so gross!—and there you were cleaning up after me. I suppose that is one definition of true love: happily cleaning up the other person's most potent bodily fluids. Ha!

But every time I think of you suffering—and how you hated seeing yourself weak—it's unbearable. Those horrible Memory Care Units. You falling six times in one night and me finding you on the floor of the bathroom. Staying by your side until you and the staff forced me to go home and sleep. They were so afraid I would get sick and die before you. But I'm still here, sweetheart, and you are gone.

You were a gentleman to the very end.

I love you with all my heart, all my soul, and all my might.

Your Dearest Darling,

Estrella

6

MY JIM,

I try to keep myself busy, but when I walk by your picture, the tears pour out of me.

I hold your picture against my heart and kiss you and send you all the love I can.

It is so painful to be without you. I pray I will make it through these dark moments.

I read your letter all the time. I worry taking it out of my wallet and unfolding it and folding it so much will make it tear or fade. But I cannot help myself.

I'm watching *Shtisel* again to distract myself, but soon I will go to bed. And cry again.

If only I could touch you one more time. Dear G-d help me through this.

Your Dearest Darling,

Estrella

7

My Dear Sweet Jim,

Today I went to a Chinese market to buy a couple things. One was marinated plums. I had an urge for some, for something to calm me down.

I don't know if I ever told you about this. When I was growing up and going to Mexico City to visit family for the summer, I used to go to the corner store and buy marinated plums, which they kept on the counter in a large jar. We paid like five Mexican cents, which wasn't even an American penny for each plum. Today they cost twelve dollars (!!) at the Chinese store, so I didn't get them, but I did get some dried chrysanthemums. Good for stress.

I made dinner/lunch and ate at 3pm, just like I used to eat in Mexico. There they eat their heavy meal between two o'clock and three o'clock and I made *enchiladas de mole*, which is the peanut butter/chocolate sauce, very good. I don't eat like Americans eat. No three meals a day.

I've always liked the Mexican way. They take a siesta after their heavy lunch and I may just do the same, but I wanted to write to you first. I promised myself that I wouldn't turn on the TV until this evening to watch *Shtesil*. I don't think it's good to binge!

Alright darling, I'm going to take my siesta, I'll continue later.

Darling,

When I woke up, I swam in our lap pool. It was a little cool, but very refreshing. I texted Rosemary to let her know I was going in. Even though she's three hours away, it gives me peace of mind and I know you would want me to be safe.

As soon as I started my laps, all I could do was cry. It doesn't seem fair that you were taken from me. I am angry at G-d for doing this, and yet I'm supposed to love him unconditionally. How? You're up there with him now. Can you tell me... is he angry with me?

Your Dearest Darling,

Estrella

8

Sweet Jim,

I went to Nellie's this morning. I wasn't sure I would be able to go there again, since it was your favorite place for breakfast and we were there together so many times and every inch of that place reminds me of you. But somehow I managed to go.

As I was parking, I saw our friend Charlie leaving. I waved at him and called out, but you know he has a problem hearing, so he didn't turn around. I ordered my scrambled eggs and English muffin with coffee and saw that none of our friends were there, so I asked this lady if I could sit with her and she was so nice and said yes.

She introduced herself and said I used to be her massage therapist. Talk about kismet! Her name is Liz, and she was so complimentary about my work and said I helped her a lot. She was so happy I asked to sit with her. She's going through a hard time with her husband in the hospital, and we just sat there and supported each other. She took my phone number and will contact me as a friend, not for a massage, because you know I retired ten years ago.

It was through your support and love that I even became a massage therapist. I so wish I would have given you more massages, but you knew how tired I would get and you never made me feel guilty for not working more on you. But I did cut your hair every four or five weeks.

There is nothing I would rather do tonight than cut your hair and sweep it all up off the floor.

And then I would give you SUCH a massage.

Your Dearest Darling,

Estrella

9

My Dearest Darling,

That's what you always called me. "Dearest Darling." Even before we got married.

Forty-two times, in fact.

Remember I took Marc to Israel when he was eleven, so he could develop an appreciation for his roots? But the trip was also an excuse for me to get away from you, because I was so scared about leaving my first marriage. How could I leave a 21-year marriage? I ran away from you, all the way to Israel, but you gave me 42 cards to take with me, all of them starting with... "My Dearest Darling."

When I returned from Israel and said "no" to you, my resolve lasted only two weeks before I was back in your arms.

And then you gave me a life no money could buy, like a fairy tale. The Commander's wife in Panama. You in your Navy whites as handsome as could be. When you married me, I always wondered what I did to deserve such a life.

I have been so honored to be your wife and proud to stand next to you. Who would have thought that a Jewish/Sephardic girl would marry such a distinguished Episcopalian Naval Officer?

How I long for those days when I would make love to you. Our love-making was always beautiful and respectful. Even today at our age I would do anything to be in your arms, clinging to you with ferocious tenderness.

But all I can cling to are the memories.

Your Dearest Darling,

Estrella

10

My Dearest Jim,

I got up at 8am this morning, late for me, but it's ok. I'm not going anywhere until noon to see Shirley, my grief therapist. She's very nice and also lost her husband many years ago, so she understands the pain in my heart.

When I got up, I talked to myself and said, "Estrella, this morning, don't you cry." But here I am, the tears streaking my cheeks. It happens every time I start writing. I guess I have to let it happen. Because if I don't let it out, if I try to keep it in, I won't be able to focus on finishing all this paperwork. You wouldn't believe how much there has been, but I've got most of it done.

You're lucky you went before me. Doing all this work is awful. Sometimes I don't know where to go or where to turn.

When I was little and we used to drive from L.A. to Tijuana, because my father had business throughout Southern California and Northern Mexico, I used to see those cute sailor boys in their uniforms, but never in my mind did I know I would fall in love with one, especially an officer.

It took me almost forty years to find you. Remember the beautiful wedding cake my daughter Naomi made for us? Two hearts with "Jim" and "Estrella" in perfect cursive icing. She also made a book for your service: "Celebrating the Life of Jim Engelhardt." Thankfully, she didn't include any pictures from your last days in the hospital. For some reason today I keep thinking of how you got so confused when my son Marc visited. You thought I was leaving you for a younger man, and you were so distraught you tried to hurt yourself, but that just landed you in the hospital and then things got *really* shitty. You went from one memory care to another. Never enough staff or dignity. Those images are stuck in my head and I have to live with them.

I'm sorry I had to put you there, but you were a big man and I couldn't do it alone. I'm sorry. I'm sorry.

Oh my love, I'm so so sorry.

Your Dearest Darling,

Estrella

11

My dearest Jim,

I just got back from my counseling session with Shirley. She's so easy to talk with and a very sweet person who lost her husband at age 50. Not everyone understands what we go through. Only those who have had a "soulmate" can fathom the deep pain we feel when losing our loved one.

I spoke to her about James, your son who loves me and appreciates the time I take to email him. I tell him it's two sided, because writing him helps me a lot in my sadness and loneliness. He is so kind. You should be very proud of him. We write every evening and it helps me handle my pain.

The twenty-plus years that you two didn't communicate were not a waste. He's getting to know you through me and I am more than happy to give him this gift.

I also spoke with Shirley about "push buttons." She was scandalized, but we laughed. What I wouldn't give to have one more afternoon in an hourly Love Motel with you. You always could push my buttons...

Aching for you.

Your Dearest Darling,

Estrella

12

My Darling Jim,

This afternoon I went to the National Cremation Society to pick up the amended death certificate. Hopefully, the VA will accept it and forward me your pension. Every time I have to do something regarding your passing, I break out in tears.

I also got a card with some beautiful words from Blue Skies of Texas regarding senior living for Military, Police, and Firefighters. I'm not making any decisions for a year, maybe more, but I'm going to go see it. They give me three nights free and all the meals I can eat, so I'll consider it a mini-vacation. I don't like the idea of leaving our home, because I'm surrounded by your love and all the beautiful things you've made through the years. Every day I look at them, especially the jewelry case and hamper in the bathroom. Those and the tile table in the living room are my favorites.

I miss you so much, my love. Sometimes I wonder if all this will be less painful as time goes by. But also—is this strange?—I don't want the pain to end. I don't want this state of being without you to become normal. The pain is an echo of your love.

If the pain goes away, will I miss it the way I miss you?

Your Dearest Darling,

Estrella

13

My Beloved Jim,

Two weeks before you went to Heaven—because I know your soul went there—our dear friend Craig, the owner of Nellie's Deli, passed away. His wife found him in his desk chair. Must've been the shock of her life. Poor Fredda, she had to take the business over and hasn't had a chance to mourn his passing.

About ten days ago she finally had a memorial service for Craig, and I met a very nice Rabbi who conducted the service. Fredda introduced me to him and he invited me to his Temple. I could not go last Saturday, but I went today. The service was an hour and a half long and the discussion following was another hour. There was an Oneg Shabbat afterwards where they served food that Fredda had contributed from Nellie's Deli.

I spent hours there, and just before I left I said goodbye to the Rabbi. He escorted me out. He's not pushing me to come back, but he said I was always welcome and I thought he was very kind.

Oops! My cell phone rang. When I checked it, I saw your picture because it's always on my screen as the wallpaper. And then I couldn't help myself. I opened my phone and looked at your picture and many others of you at Nellie's, so of course I started crying and hugging the phone. There were also those pictures of you in your uniform at the Veteran's Day function at the elementary school. I remember all the children saluting you and I was so proud of you and how handsome you looked in your Commander's uniform.

All my love.

Your Dearest Darling,

Estrella

14

Dearest Jim,

It's after 9pm, but I had to tell you something really quick before going to bed.

I just finished watching *Shtisel*. Tonight an episode mentioned Bnai Brak, and my memory time-traveled to 1981. See, I spent a Sabbath at Bnai Brak one time, all those years ago, during my six-week trip to Israel with my son Marc. When I returned from that trip, I told you I couldn't marry you. An Orthodox Rabbi in Israel had told me I had to try to mend fences with my first husband. I can still see so clearly the devastation in your face, but also your resolve.

Thank G-d it didn't last! So what if you weren't Jewish? I would have missed the forty years of wonderful things we had together out of some ridiculous sense of "guilt."

That's what I had to tell you. As painful as all this is, I wouldn't trade it. The pain is the price for the joy we shared.

Your Dearest Darling,

Estrella

15

Dearest Sweet Jim,

I just sent off an email to your son, James. He is such a good support person for me, and I for him. He doesn't say much except how much he appreciates my writing to him every day. He is hurting so much for having lost you.

I believe a loss like this hurts a lot more when you've let years go by without communication. I cried when my parents died, especially for my Mother who lived with us the last three years of her life, but at least I had closure with them.

Remember the times you came home from work and Mother was sitting on the living room couch? You would sit next to her and put your arm around her and say, "Have you been a good girl today?" She would laugh so much.

You also introduced her to cosmopolitans! I remember the day we went to the steakhouse, and you lifted her up on the bar stool and ordered the drink. She liked it so much she ordered a second one. Of course, she was tiny, not even 5 feet tall, so those two were more than enough!

How I long for those days. It was a privilege to take care of both of you.

I hope you two are enjoying cosmopolitans together right now. Surely Heaven has good bartenders!

Your Dearest Darling,

Estrella

16

Dear Sweet Jim,

I just finished cleaning the pool patio with the broom and hose, and it looks nice out there. While I was cleaning, I had music playing. "Annie Get Your Gun" with Howard Keel and Betty Hutton. When Howard Keel started singing "The Girl That I Marry," I cried so hard I had to turn it off. Our marriage was like a fantasy that you see on the screen, except it was real. I remember you taking me to all those embassy parties in Panama. I would dress in beautiful long summer gowns because it was always hot. You would tell people how I would slither out of the car and look so very sexy and beautiful. Until you told me, I didn't believe it.

But as wonderful as Panama was, what I cherish even more are the 38 years we shared in our little house in Sarasota.

Every day I marvel at all the beautiful pieces you made from wood. I am surrounded by your love.

Well, darling, I've procrastinated enough and I do have to get my paperwork done. My friend Rosemary comes next Friday and I want to get it done before she arrives. I have two tickets for a cabaret show at the theatre. I hope I can be kind to myself and not make a scene crying, because that was something you and I loved to do.

G-d Bless you, my beloved husband.

Your Dearest Darling,

Estrella

17

Dearest Jim,

Just when I thought I was getting stronger, I see your picture on the counter. Then I get sad and sit on the pillows where I sat Shiva for you. I play "You Raise Me Up" by Josh Groban and the tears flow. In a way it helps so I can get on with my work. Those words "You raise me up so I can stand on mountains, you raise me up to walk on stormy seas, I am strong when I am on your shoulders, you raise me up to more than I can be."

Let me break this down for you.

You raise me up so I can stand on mountains. I have this mental picture of a powerful woman standing on the edge of a mountain saying, "Look at me, how strong I am."

You raise me up to walk on stormy seas. I remember so many stories of you being in typhoons and knowing how to navigate the ship and keeping your men safe, but for me, it's navigating my life through these stormy times and how your love has made me strong.

I am strong when I am on your shoulders. I don't feel so strong, because you're not here to guide me, yet I know I have to be strong for myself and those people that love me.

You raise me up to more than I can be. That part really resonates with me. You once said you worried about me being too dependent on you, and even too "clingy," but you helped me become successful in so many things I tried. I may not have made a lot of money—in fact I spend a lot, as you know!—but everything I did, from dancing and acting to doing transformational workshops and becoming a Licensed Massage Therapist, I did because I had you there supporting me and making me feel I could do anything I set my mind to. You helped me to go for it!

I cannot tell you how much you mean to me.

Your Dearest Darling,

Estrella

18

Darling Jim,

I'm listening to some beautiful Spanish guitar that you used to love. I had to put something beautiful on, because I'm filling out some paperwork about you, and it says "deceased." It's torture.

I've done a little of the work I'm supposed to complete, but I get sidetracked a lot. You always told me to make a list and sometimes I do, but today I didn't and it's like I'm all over the place.

I've been going through Israeli dances on the internet to see how many I can remember, then I watched some flamenco, and finally came across this beautiful Spanish guitar. I can't say I've totally wasted a whole day, but I did get distracted by other things instead of taking care of this awful paperwork. Oh well, there is always tomorrow.

Except... maybe there's not. A tomorrow, I mean. How are we to know?

This paperwork is for insurance, so they can compensate me with a small policy. Every penny counts, but I'd give it all up just to have you with me. My heart aches to hear your voice or to touch you. Pictures just don't cut it.

There go the tears again. The Spanish guitarist just finished playing "I Can't Stop Loving You." It's true. I can't. I won't. I never will.

Your Dearest Darling,

Estrella

19

My Darling Jim,

I woke up crying again. What do I have to do, take away all your pictures? I won't do that. My eyes have bags under them from crying so much. I know there are other people suffering the loss of their loved one like me, but still I feel alone.

I've been breaking out in rashes. First it was the upper left shoulder and below, then it was my scalp, then my arms, now my lower back and even my left leg. What is happening to me? I know it's all the stress I went through and the loneliness I feel without you. I have to get better.

I'm trying to decide whether to meditate, swim, or go to Nellie's. If I go to Nellie's I'll see friends, but if I meditate, it might give me some relief. Of course, swimming is good for me, too.

Hmmmm.

I'm back. I meditated. And then I went to Nellie's. I sat with Charlie, who is a happy camper with Susan. They fulfill each other and I'm very happy for them. Of course, we talked about food and I told him he would enjoy watching *Somebody Feed Phil*. You would have enjoyed it a lot. This Jewish guy goes all over the world and tastes the food of each country. He's always very complimentary of everything they feed him. Yesterday he did an episode in Mexico City. I loved it! It conjured memories of my youth, all except the part where he ate ants and worms. The ants were ground up and so were the worms, but still. Blech! And not very Kosher.

Tomorrow I'm going to the VA. I hope it's positive and they give me your VA pension. I'll believe it when I see it.

I also received another email from number one son James. He is such a kind soul, just like his dad.

Your Dearest Darling,

Estrella

20

My Darling Jim,

Today was a busy day. I exercised my arms, meditated, looked at paperwork that needs my attention, and then at one I had an appointment with the Veteran's Administration to give the information on the Amended Burial Certificate. Nothing is finalized, but hopefully they will continue sending me your VA pension, which will help me take care of our finances and run our home satisfactorily.

The pool guy checked the motor and said I have to replace it to the tune of $425. That's what I mean about running our home. I know we have monies to help me out, but having the VA pension will take away a lot of stress.

I actually had to go back twice, because there were other papers I forgot to bring in, but it's all handled. Now I wait for their decision.

This morning—big surprise—I woke up and cried. It doesn't seem to end. Part of me understands this is difficult. Part of me wishes I could get over this. But if I get over it, does that mean I've stopped loving you?

You have been and will always be the man who stole my heart. I know it's awful, but when I'm out running errands or sitting at Nellie's, I look at older men and think, "Why are they living and not my Jim?" I'm so sorry if that makes you sad. Some people tell me if I cry, I'm making you sad. How the hell do they know? Have they been to Heaven and come back? NO! Sometimes I don't know what's real, but I know I love you more than anything. I also know I feel sorry for myself, but I don't know if that's selfish.

Your Dearest Darling,

Estrella

21

Dearest Jim,

Last night I had a dream about Sherry and Cy, your best friend. Cy is not well and I'm sure he'll be joining you soon. I don't know if I will have it in me to be as supportive and loving as Sherry has been to me, but it looks like we'll all have to go through this sadness to reach another dimension, if you believe in those things. I want to, because I so much want to see you again.

The dream was going to Clearwater and walking on the beach with Cy and Sherry. Then we all went to a restaurant, and there was a band playing Irish music.

I hate to tell you this, but your number one son James is not doing too well. I want so much to help him and I don't know what to do. He's between insurances and transitioning to Medicaid since he doesn't have money. I wish you were here to tell me what to do. I know you would want to help and so do I.

Even though he's struggling, he sent me a beautiful prayer called "Inner Peace." It goes like this:

I enter my inner sanctuary and breathe in peace.

Inner peace is a sanctuary I can enter at any time.

Just knowing this space exists within me helps me feel grounded and secure.

When I focus my attention on the rhythm of my breathing, my body begins to settle.

All my worries and tension fall away like sand descending to the bottom of a lake, leaving behind clear, placid water.

I enter my inner sanctuary where everything is still, and I breathe in the serenity.

He is such a sweet soul. He reminds me so much of you. He didn't know I was born in Mexico. He loves that I write to him and tells me I am his friend, that there is no one else that he can be so open with. I will help him as much as I can. There was a lot of sadness between the two of you. I can't fathom not talking with my children for over thirty years, but how wonderful that we got in touch with him before you left us and he could tell you he always loved you. That was a big deal for him.

He told me he loves to cook and fish and so did you. Maybe he can get a job as a chef. Do you remember Percy, our Argentinian friend? He's a chef at a retirement center. I'm going to call him and see if he has any suggestions. I would be glad to have James stay here until he's able to get on his feet. What do you think about that? I wouldn't be so lonely, but he would have to be clean like you! Sometimes I get sloppy, but I know you're in Heaven watching me, so I make sure our home looks clean and beautiful.

Kisses and hugs to you, my husband.

Your Dearest Darling,

Estrella

22

My Darling Jim,

When I sit at the desk you made for me, here in my office, with the massage table you made for me against the wall, and all 42 cards you wrote for me when I went to Israel right here within reach, all of it so well made and written with lots of love... do you see? I'm always embraced by you.

Did you know I read all 42 of those cards on the plane ride over? I couldn't wait. Even though you wrote me one for each day I would be away—7 days a week times 6 weeks—I couldn't save any for later. I was ready to tell the pilot to turn the plane around right then and there. Instead, I had six weeks with my son in Israel, and listened to the Rabbi, and came home and told you no. But I held on to the cards. Because somehow I knew—I always knew—that our story had only begun.

And these letters I write to you continue our story. I pray you feel my love, because as I write, I feel like I'm with you.

What a lazy day for me. I can't seem to get my other paperwork done. The most important ones are finished. It's just that the mail comes and I get more to look through. I would rather write to you. I promise I will get it handled tomorrow for sure.

There is a Facebook page I found. It's widows who have lost their loved ones. I write to them as well.

It seems I'm often writing, so I'm not wasting time. I'm just going in another direction.

But now I must do some work, because you know how messy my office gets and Friday I'll have company. Rosemary is coming over, and then we are going to the cabaret, which you and I used to enjoy so much together. I wonder how I'll react without you there? Hopefully, I won't embarrass Rosemary or myself. Or you!

Your Dearest Darling,

Estrella

23

Dearest Jim,

Although I got distracted temporarily with *Somebody Feed Phil*, it's bedtime for me.

Every night, just before I go to bed, I kiss your pictures and take your letter out of my wallet and read it and then fold it back up and put it back and then I kiss your pictures again.

Getting into bed is awful. It's too big. It doesn't feel right. I refuse to sleep in the middle. I stay on my side and throw my arm across hoping it will land on your chest, but it never does.

I hope you will visit me in my dreams.

Your Dearest Darling,

Estrellla

24

My Dearest Jim,

I started exercising my flabby arms to this beautiful bolero. I have a love for dancing that I've not been able to express in a long time and it is important that I do. I so wanted you to be a good dancer, but there came a time when it wasn't important. Now that I'm alone, I am gravitating to that passion again. I would love to help others learn the beautiful Latin dances. It's not important that I make money out of it, but it's important that I find someone who will partner with me and dance, dance, dance.

As I was dancing, it felt so good. I actually found myself smiling. And then immediately I felt guilty about enjoying myself and thinking about dancing with a partner, because you were always my #1. And I was yours.

I stopped dancing. I made a snack and put on YouTube and tried to distract myself from the guilt. And then WOW. Did I ever get a wake-up call! I came across Matthew McConaughey's motivational speech when he received his Oscar. It was about appreciating oneself and did it ever call to me. I think maybe you might have reached down and guided the YouTube for me.

I've been writing these letters to you to avoid feeling lonely and to remind myself of how you loved me. And in his speech Matthew said it's ok to do that, but first you need to sit with yourself and like who you are. It's the same story that if you can't love yourself, how can you love others? I really heard it this time, and if I can put it into practice, I really think I will be more than ok. I will be more than I knew I could be.

Thank you, my love, for your guidance and helping me see I am worthwhile.

You will always be my #1.

Your Dearest Darling,

Estrella

25

My Darling Jim,

Today I went to Nellie's for coffee, and Bob was sitting by himself. I know you two never really got along, but I didn't feel like sitting alone, so I asked if I could sit with him. He said of course. Turns out he's a kind man with many problems. I left and started sobbing in the car. Don't worry, darling, I am a safe driver and keep in control. I got home and sat on the pillows where I sat Shiva for you and played "You Raise Me Up," so I can get my crying out of the way and focus on things that have to be done.

I went to Facebook and chatted with other weeping widows. It helps, a little. Then I had lunch and got ready to see Shirley, my grief counselor. But before I did, I made a list so that I would remember to cover all the points I wanted to discuss with her. Shirley is glad that I have a very loving relationship with number one son James. I write emails to him at least twice a day, and he answers, usually in short little sentences, but that's ok. He also includes happy faces and hearts.

I told him about the beautiful woodwork that surrounds me with your love every day. The beautiful dining room table you made. The hutches. The queen-size bed. My favorite pieces are the tile coffee table, the hamper in the bathroom, my jewelry box, my massage table, and this very desk I sit at when I write you.

I also bought a book on tape. It's Matthew McConaughey's life story, and he narrates it. It's six hours long and I've listened to about half. I actually stayed awake to hear it, not like so many other times when we used to listen to books and I would fall asleep so you would have to clue me in. His Oscar speech really touched me.

I laid down for a little siesta the way we used to do together and when I got up, there came the tears. Do you know I take your gorgeous picture in uniform and I lay it next to me in bed? I feel safe knowing you're laying next to me. It may sound strange, but who cares.

Your Dearest Darling,

Estrella

26

My Darling Jim,

It's a Tuesday, just two months and seven days since you went to Heaven. You'd think by this point the tears would let up some, but it's bullshit. I cry just as much as the moment the hospice nurse told me you were gone.

I hated those moments when you were under their care. I should have been caring for you. But it was impossible. I could see in your eyes that you were begging me for water, but they told me if I gave you water you would aspirate and have a painful death, because whatever you drank would go into your lungs. How does one deal with that? What choice did I have? The morphine was to make it easier on you, and I would have given you all of it, but they wouldn't up the dose. Did they kill you? Did I?

So many questions. So many painful images. Forgive me, my darling, I was only following instructions and I'll have to deal with the pain of your sad eyes for the rest of my life.

Everyone says how strong I am, but I don't feel strong at all. I keep listening to Josh Groban's song "You Raise Me Up." Because that's what you did for me. But your passing has pushed me down and I'm sick and tired of people telling me I am strong. NO! I am not. Or if I am, or ever was, then I've forgotten what strength feels like, and I have no idea how to remember.

This is my time to weep and scream. I'm so sorry, but sometimes I'm furious at you for leaving me.

I just got a phone call from our investment company and, poor guy, the moment I said my husband recently passed away, I started crying. He asked if he should call back or send me an email about our investments. I just don't know what to do. If you were here, you would tell me, but I have to make all these decisions and "grow up."

I'm still battling a rash. At first, Dr. Joe said it was shingles and gave me some horrible medication that made me nauseous and sleepy, and I told him so. I saw another doctor who said it wasn't shingles. I had two vaccinations recently for that condition. The dermatologist said it was neuro-dermatitis. It is a real pain. Oh yes, Dr. Cao, our acupuncturist, gave me a treatment and some cream. Nothing works, except a Claritin every 24 hours, but I want this gone before I visit Blue Skies and see Marc in Austin and Naomi in California.

Remember I mentioned I want to get back to teaching dance? Well, I discovered that I have at least fifteen dances that I remember! I have always loved to dance, but my father's voice—*nice girls don't perform*—has so many times gotten in the way. I also have to get myself back in shape. I lost twenty pounds from the stress I've gone through these past six months, so my weight is good. Now I have to work on stamina.

Your Dearest Darling,

Estrella

27

Darling Jim,

Tell me all about Heaven. Have you connected with your parents? My parents? All your dear friends, especially Donnie, whom you always said was your best friend?

I have an idea for a story. "Nellie's Friends." So many of us have been loyal customers for almost twenty years. That's a long time for restaurant friends. I still go there two or three times a week and sit with either Charlie, Phyllis, Peter, or whoever else is there.

They have new people working there. Alex and Hannah are gone. Alex got a job at a country club in Lakewood Ranch and Hannah... huh. I actually don't know.

The coffee is still the best in town, and the bagels are wonderful. I had two in the past two days. I have to be careful, don't want to put the weight on again. When I go to Texas and California to see family I want to look good!

I've been swimming in our lap pool and doing arm exercises with some three-pound weights, but I have to be careful. They started hurting my neck and shoulder. Can't have that.

It's noon and I'm still in pajamas. I need to take a bath, wash my hair, get ready to go to the bank, and then see Dr. Cao.

You would be so proud of me. I'm keeping the plants watered and the patio nice and clean.

Your Dearest Darling,

Estrella

28

My Darling Jim,

I heard the gardener outside. That must mean it's Wednesday. Days all blend.

I went to Nellie's and sat with Charlie. He is a very kind person. Today he was complaining about what I thought were little things, but then I stopped and thought that wasn't fair of me. After all, what's little to me might be big to him. Would someone walking past me on the street know the depths of the pain I'm currently going through? We just don't really know much about each other. That's one of the biggest reasons I miss you: you KNEW me. With you gone, now I feel unknown.

When Charlie left, I went and sat with Peter and Phyllis. They are also very nice and helpful. Phyllis knows a lot about investing, but don't worry. I will not do anything crazy.

I left Nellie's and went to Office Max to fax some information to the long-term care company. The fax would not go through, so I had to come home and get another number they gave me. If I had listened to my gut, I would have taken both numbers the first time, but I didn't. So I had to come back home and get it. It finally went through and they will re-send the corrected check.

I went to Publix and bought some lettuce, sour cream, and watermelon. I made some delicious green enchiladas and maybe I'll have company for dinner. I love you and miss you and wish you were here, but I have to understand that you're not and accept the reality that G-d has taken you home.

I really hope that's true. Sometimes I don't know if I believe all that.

I listened in bed last night to Matthew McConaughey's book on tape, *Greenlights*. He narrates so well I got all caught up and didn't realize it was 11pm! I turned it off and wouldn't you know it, I slept deeply and woke at my normal time. I did, however, have a strange dream. You and I were at a resort and had our baby boy with us, the baby we never had.

I married you when I was forty and I could not have any more children. My tubes had been tied. If we'd had a baby, they'd be almost forty today. Of course you brought five kids into our marriage and I brought two. I think that was enough!

My emails to number one son James are very kind and appreciative. He helps me fight my loneliness and I do the same for him, writing to him every day. He is his daddy's son. He texted me because I sent him that beautiful picture of us, you in your mess dress and I in a beautiful gown. We both are amazed at how he looks just like you.

Your Dearest Darling,

Estrella

.

29

Dear Sweet Jim,

Charlie and his brother Frank were here for dinner. I made green enchiladas, refried beans, and rice. They ate it all!

Frank is having a hip replacement. He's only 70 and Charlie is 73. We are lucky not to have such problems.

But hearing about medical stuff brought up all these horrible memories. Like the stubborn doctor who took you off your memantine medicine and put you on ketamine, because he didn't think you had dementia and wanted to treat you for PTSD. The medicine he gave you made you hallucinate. You thought I was going to divorce you and run off with a younger man. They say that everything is pre-arranged by G-d. What a shitty pre-arrangement that was, but are we supposed to question it? I don't know. I'm still so angry that you had to go through that.

Let's get off that subject. Today I'm going to see Sofia, the nurse practitioner. She put me on a medication for my anxiety, but I never took it. I don't want any drugs to suppress the sadness and loneliness I feel. It's all a part of the grieving experience and if I have to cry three or four times a day, so be it.

Last night was the first night that number one son James didn't write to me. I hope he's ok. I want to call him today, but I'm concerned I may be pushing him too much. So much wasted time between the two of you. But, again, if it was preordained, what could you have done?

Your Dearest Darling,

Estrella

30

My Dearest Jim,

Today I went to Costco, and I saw a bunch of older men with white hair, and again I got so sad and asked G-d, "Why are they alive and not my Jim?!" I got in the car and screamed my head off. I hope I'm not making you sad, but sometimes this pain I feel is unbearable.

People have no idea what it's like to lose your soulmate and best friend, and I don't wish this on anyone. There is simply no way to prepare anyone for this. I wish I could help others, but right now I have to go through this by myself and pray that I'll come out stronger for it, and then maybe I will find a way to help others.

I am also a little concerned because number one son James did not write to me yesterday or today. I hope I'm not pushing him too hard to keep in touch with me.

I think I'm going to watch a movie on Netflix. Naomi told me about one with Sandra Bullock. We don't always agree on movies, but the last one we did. That was also Sandra Bullock. *Miss Congeniality 2*. We both laughed a lot. Some laughter tonight would be good.

Your Dearest Darling,

Estrella

31

Dearest Jim,

Another morning I wake to a half-empty bed.

I had a strange dream last night. We were in a place that looked like a desert. There were mountains and an ocean and I had driven into this place, but it looked abandoned, many mansions, but no one around. I wanted to get out of there, but I didn't know my way out. So I latched on to the outside of this bus loaded with Mexican workers and thought they would help me out of there. There was one mean guy who I thought would throw me off, but he had pity on me and didn't. Then the dream switched over to an enormous outside restaurant where people were eating whatever they could get, and I went around with a big green trash bag cleaning up after them. The sky was red. I came back to where you were sitting and made sure you were getting something to eat. Then I woke up.

I don't know that it "means" anything. But it was wonderful to see you in my dream, and it's wonderful to tell you about it, even though it was bizarre.

At 3pm I went to see Dr. Cao to try to get rid of my rash. It's doing better and hopefully gone before I go to Texas and California. Please tell G-d to keep us safe from any and all illness when we travel. I want to be as healthy as possible.

Do you remember the wonderful time we went to celebrate my 75th birthday in Palm Desert? Naomi and you threw a wonderful party for me. I have the book and pictures that Naomi had printed out for us. She also made the beautiful book to celebrate your life. It's on the gorgeous tile table you made for us.

Maybe the dream was your way of letting me know that you're watching over me. Could I ask for more pleasant dreams? You know I scare easy. I used to jump when you would walk up behind me in the kitchen, and the solution you came up with was to ring the little bell we have on the counter.

Fill my dreams with bells, my love, so I know you're close behind me.

Your Dearest Darling,

Estrella

32

My Dearest Jim,

I keep writing these letters for various reasons.

First, you are always in my heart and I am with you a little more intimately when I write.

Second, there are no quick fixes to the grief, pain, and sadness I feel having lost you. Writing about those feelings gets them out, makes them smaller or at least more manageable. By saying it, I can hold it, instead of being paralyzed by it. I will continue to write, my darling. It keeps me "anchored." (Did you like my little Navy joke, my handsome sailor??)

Third, perhaps someday others will read these letters, and gain some measure of solace from recognizing in me a kindred spirit. Someone who shares their burden. Who lets them know they are not alone, even though it feels like it.

And last, I write because every time I take out from my wallet the love letter you wrote me, and go back over all those promises you made, I am compelled to respond.

Jim, you fulfilled all your promises, and while we are no longer together in the flesh, you are always, always in my heart.

Thank you.

Your Dearest Darling,

Estrella

33

My Dearest Jim,

This may make you angry or afraid, but sometimes I get bad thoughts in my head. The pain feels so unbearable that I think about how to end it. Feeling nothing seems like paradise compared to the daily agony of this empty house.

I wouldn't ever follow through with these thoughts, because I know I would hurt many people, and they don't need to go through the pain or embarrassment of me doing something wrong.

But there. I said it. I'm sure many other widows or widowers have had these thoughts, but no one—not even me—expresses them in all the Facebook posts from my buddies. Yes, they're my buddies. I feel their pain, their sadness, their grief, and we are—as someone put it a few months ago—"the club no one wants to belong to."

I just took out the trash. I keep on doing my chores and wonder what the hell is this all for?

Your number one son James has stopped writing. Was I too pushy or maybe too clingy? I remember you telling me when we first started going together that I scared you because I was too clingy. Could I have scared him? I hope not. He was helping me feel stronger and suddenly he stops writing.

There's that ugly "abandonment" issue popping up for me. I may have said this before, but I've carried this feeling of abandonment with me most of my life. But then you came into my life and I felt I was worth something. With you gone, am I still worth something?

Everyone looks at me with pity. It's awful. I don't feel seen. Their pity is a shield. It protects them from the real, blunt, raw truth of me.

And I never could have guessed how simply not having your eyes on me would make me feel so invisible. If I'm already invisible anyway, then why not follow through on those bad thoughts?

Your letter keeps me from acting. And your picture. You're not here, but I cling to you.

Your Dearest Darling,

Estrella

34

My Darling Jim,

Yesterday I went with a friend to see a movie. I had not been to a movie theatre for four years and didn't really miss it, but they had these great recliners and it was very nice. The same kind of seats they have at that theatre where they serve you a full dinner. Remember when we went, and you ordered a Korean dish that spilled all over your lap? I felt so bad for you, because it was at the beginning of the film and you had to sit there with that mess throughout the entire movie. But oh did you smell spicy all night, delicious man.

Today I wrote to my cousin in Israel. She is a wise woman, and I told her about my guilt for letting the neurologist take you off the dementia medication. He put you on ketamine, which caused you to take actions that landed you in the hospital. Then the Memory Care units. Then more and more downhill. You never wanted to end up in such places, because you saw Grandma Alice going through the same thing and her family had to place her in similar care.

It is so difficult to get rid of this guilt. And this anger at the doctor. And this rage at your illness.

I have asked my cousin's advice and will await an answer, as she has always given me good counsel.

Darling, I ask your forgiveness in this matter as it consumes my life.

I'm going to go to bed thinking of that mess in your lap, remembering being at the movies with you.

Your Dearest Darling,

Estrella

35

Dearest Jim,

I went to Nellie's and sat with Charlie. He tells me nice things about his relationship with Susan and I'm so happy he's found his soulmate. I know what it's like since you are my soulmate and I love you more than anything in the world. No one will ever take your place.

Of course I was crying when I got home, but before I walked into our house I said to myself, "You have work to do, so get it done today."

I made an appointment to see my chiropractor, which I've been putting off for a long time since going there makes me so sad, because you always came with me and sat in one of the chairs in the lobby while he took about ten minutes to adjust my spine. There's a pain in my neck and I think using the three-pound weights may have caused it. I'm working on toning my arms so that I can wear sleeveless blouses and not have saggy triceps.

Meanwhile, I wrote down things I have to do, which helps me stay focused. You taught me how to do that. I think of you watching me from Heaven and guiding me. Are you? Do you?

The battery-powered candles go on by themselves every night and I feel your presence. You bought those candles. You put those batteries in. Oh no! When those batteries die, the candles won't come on. When I replace those batteries, I will lose another little piece of you.

How can the world just keep moving on without you?

Your Dearest Darling,

Estrella

36

My Darling Jim,

This morning, my cousin from Israel emailed me back. She is so wise and kind. She told me that crying too much doesn't help elevate your soul, so I will try not to cry as much. I want your soul elevated as high as it can go. One of these days mine will be right there with yours.

She also told me to stop feeling guilty about taking you to the neurologist that I put so much blame on for the awful pain of your final days. Easier said than done.

She was also smart enough not to ask me how I am. People are always asking me how I am. I hate that, but it's just something they say, and I get triggered. If I were blunt I would say, "How the hell do you think I am? I am grieving my husband!" But I don't. I usually just say, "Y'know. Getting there."

Getting there??? Getting WHERE? Getting to a point where I don't grieve as much? How long does that take?

Please tell me you are elevating. Please tell me you forgive me for crying so much.

Your Dearest Darling,

Estrella

37

Dearest Jim,

I still write to number one son James, but he hasn't answered for a week. It sucks, just when we were having a very sweet relationship. So I wrote to him and said he doesn't have to answer, but that I'm here whenever he wants to talk. You know I have trouble when people play the silent game with me. I'd rather someone just say "f—k off" if that's what they want.

Maybe I confused him. Who knows, maybe he's embarrassed and feels sick. I don't understand. There's so much I don't understand.

The candles still go on by themselves. I know it's just batteries. But I like to think you're here.

Your Dearest Darling,

Estrella

38

My Dearest Jim,

Sundays are the hardest. Everybody is busy with their own lives, and I am here alone, feeling sorry for myself. How pathetic is that? I have got to change my thinking. Let's see. It's Sunday. Which means no one is going to bother me. So I can get things done. Does that sound a little better?

I have Dean Martin playing. He's singing *Arrivederci Roma*. Did you know I was in Rome four times? What a crazy city! The Italian drivers are insane, but I still had so much fun being there. I imagined the gladiators in the Coliseum with the lions. Today, who are the Romans? They're the Italians!

Ever since I did my ancestry test and discovered I am 26% Italian, I understand why I have such a connection to that culture. One of the first dances I did was the Tarantella when I was about fifteen. Let me take that back. The first dances were Hawaiian. I went to the library and learned by reading about all the beautiful Hawaiian arm and hand movements, then danced for my parents' synagogue at one of their dinners.

I'm going to go take my olive oil and lemon juice right now, because I'm getting hungry and I do that first. Then I take my other morning pills that have to be taken before I eat. I'll be back later, darling.

OK, I did the above and more. I swam my laps, laid ten minutes in the sun, came back in, and took a shower. I stripped the bed and washed the sheets. I treated myself with two fluffy buttermilk pancakes and an egg and it was delicious.

Oh boy, my eyelids are getting heavy. I better lay down and take a little nap and dream of your arms enfolding me. See you in a little while.

I laid down for about forty-five minutes, and got up crying. What's the matter with me? I've cried a lot, but never like this. Could it be that I'm going to stop soon and G-d has me literally sobbing my heart out? I don't know.

Well, my sweetheart, the sheets are dry and ready for me to make the bed, so I'll end this letter right now and get some work done. I love you more than anything and miss you tremendously.

Your Dearest Darling,

Estrella

39

My Darling Jim,

Today I got up and within fifteen minutes I was doing my laps, crying a little, but getting my exercise. Then I showered and made some breakfast and was out by 9:30 to get a cup of coffee at Nellies, and Charlie, Happy, and Cappy were there.

I came home and brought in the mail. Another letter from DFAS about "survivor's benefits." It seems they need more information so I can start receiving your Navy pay. Paperwork, paperwork, paperwork. We never talked about all the paperwork that erupts when someone passes away, but you're lucky I didn't go before you. I don't think you would have had an easy time. I haven't either, but because I'm more familiar with the computer, it's a little easier.

Also, number one son James finally replied! One reason he stopped writing is because he had to find a new place to live, and during his move his cell phone got damaged. And now he's in the hospital, but I don't know for what.

I can't seem to get a straight answer from anyone. Especially from G-d.

Your Dearest Darling,

Estrella

40

My Jim,

Today I went to see Dr. Cao who is helping me with my rash and neck pain. Afterwards I went to Nellies for a cup of coffee and Happy and Cappy were there, along with Peter and Phyllis. Cappy was so tender and said that he was glad to have known you even if it was only for one year. He really enjoyed how you two laughed together. When they left, I went and sat with Phyllis for a little while and she coached me on what to take to the financial planner who has been very good to her. I see him Thursday.

When I drove home, I noticed a light on my dashboard showing me that my left rear tire was low on air, so I took it in right away. They checked the car and put air in the tires and the sensor light went off, so all is well.

After that I went to the bank and got a little cash, came home, called the hospital where number one son James is, but he wasn't taking any calls. I will leave him alone and wait a couple of days to find out how he is. I'll pray for him in the meantime.

Then I went to Costco to get some papayas and other organic vegetables. I think I'm becoming a pescatarian. That means I don't eat meat, except for fish. I refuse to not eat fish, because the ceviche I make is too good to give up!

I got home and made dinner for myself. I had cauliflower rice, herring, broccoli, and a couple of rice crackers. I am sticking to my commitment to eat my greens every day.

The sky is black. We're going to have some rain later.

The pool is doing very well. I am keeping the patio clean.

I don't want to stop writing, even though now all I'm writing is mundane nothings. Just the stuff of a random, normal day. But sharing it with you... well, I guess the mundane becomes special. What I wouldn't give to simply watch the rain with you. Or to tidy the patio while you skimmed the pool. Such mundane nothings, but what people don't realize—what I have realized in these days without you—is that even moments of mundane nothing are unspeakably precious.

Your Dearest Darling,

Estrella

41

JIM,

Today was one of those busy, busy days. I got up, made the bed, picked up a few things, made sure I had documents ready to take to the financial advisor, went to Nellie's for my scrambled eggs, English muffin, and coffee, sat with Charlie and Happy and Cappy, said hello to Phyllis, and finally went to see the financial advisor. I had a very nice talk with him. We spoke about the money you set aside for my retirement and the best thing he suggested were CDs. They're paying 3%, so it's a safe place to put some money. I won't make a lot, but I won't lose any either.

Then I went to the International Store on Fruitville where they have Turkish coffee. I didn't get any for myself, since it gets me hyper and I already have this tremor in my thumbs and don't want to make it worse, but I bought a can for the financial advisor, since he was so nice and honest with me.

I have a couple of doctor appointments coming up. The dentist and then the ophthalmologist in the afternoon. They will dilate my eyes and although I can take an Uber, it makes me wish you were here to drive me home safely. I don't know if I'll ever get used to this, going places without you, but I am trying.

I did not take my siesta today. It's only 6pm and I'm getting sleepy, but I'm not going to bed, it's way too early. Perhaps I'll watch a movie. Or I'll go back to *Somebody Feed Phil*. He always makes me smile.

But not like you did.

Your Dearest Darling,

Estrella

42

My Dearest Jim,

Earlier today I went to the theatre to see a matinee of a cabaret show with the music of Billy Joel. I looked over to where you used to sit when we came to these shows together. How is it that absence can be such a tangible thing?

I came home and took a quick nap before my friend Patti came over with *chiles rellenos*. Then we sat down to watch *Somebody Feed Phil*. The episode was about Mexico City and it was so great. Many dishes I was unfamiliar with and others I knew. I never realized how they made churros the Mexican way: long strands of them rolled in sugar and cinnamon, and then dunked into hot chocolate. Patti is from Mexico City and shared her stories of when she was a child and her father would take them on Sundays to eat those delicious churros.

I have been dressing in black ever since you passed away, darling, and Patti suggested I wear colors, since black keeps me feeling depressed.

She said, "Jim would not like to see you that way." So I put on a shirt that was white and actually started feeling better. I have mourned you, sweet man, and have felt such pain at losing you, but I must be strong and keep on living. I know you wouldn't want your death to be the end of my life, too.

You are in bed with me every night, because I put your picture on the pillow next to me. The battery-powered lights went on again, so I will believe you came to be with me.

Your Dearest Darling,

Estrella

43

My Darling Jim,

Today I spoke with Shirley, my grief counselor, and it went well. I told her I didn't know what was happening with number one son James and that I was concerned about him, because he was in the hospital and the HIPPA law means they cannot tell me why he's there.

Then I called Ilene at Blue Skies of Texas. She will pick me up at the airport when I visit and show me around. I'm not deciding anything right away, but it will be nice to see what the place is like. It's a retirement community and only ninety minutes from Marc. But this is our home and I do not want to think of packing up the house and moving. Just looking!

And then!! I called James again tonight and this time he spoke with me! I didn't ask what happened. I just told him I loved him and he told me twice that he loved me. He is recuperating and said that I should call him whenever I want and that he's looking forward to seeing me when I go to California in October. I was so happy to hear from him. It warmed my heart.

I love you forever and ever.

Your Dearest Darling,

Estrella

44

Dearest Jim,

I had dinner at 4:45. I made the curry you taught me to make. I cried as I cooked. I cried as I ate. Aromas and flavors bring you back to me. The tears were worth it.

I talked with number one son James for a quick minute and he told me they were looking for a place for him to have rehab, so it was a little chaotic. I wished him well and told him I love him. He said to someone in the room, "That was my step-mother I was talking to. I love her."

You probably can see it all up there way before I know about it down here, but I thought you'd want to hear the good news about your son.

Your Dearest Darling,

Estrella

45

My Darling Jim,

Today I looked through my clothes to see which I will take to Texas and California and picked out some nice ones, but of course I started crying. Going anywhere without you is very painful.

In the evening, I spoke to number one son James, and he told me they were moving him into a new place to continue his rehab. They were picking him up from the hospital very late, 10:30pm. He said that's the only time the ambulance could take him. I will call him tomorrow. I also was looking at transportation from Palm Springs to his new facility and not having much luck. It's a little complicated, but I really want to work it out and see him. Otherwise he will be so disappointed. He is so very sweet, sounds like you and looks like you, only he has less hair.

I listened to more of Matthew McConaughey's book, *Greenlights*. It's an autobiography of his life and I'm enjoying it thoroughly. He is such an impressive speaker and actor. He is now my favorite. When I talk to James later, I'm going to ask him if he likes to read and send him the book. It has a lot of good advice. There's a section in the book where he talks about his trip in Peru, going down the Amazon River and also going up to Machu Picchu. Matthew took this trip because he needed a place to be without everyone recognizing him and it all started with a dream about floating down the Amazon in a raft surrounded by all kinds of dangerous animals. When he actually did it, there were no dangerous animals, but he did it with no clothes!

I'm going to look for another movie by Matthew McConaughey for tonight. If I don't find one, I'll go back to *Somebody Feed Phil*. He makes me laugh and I can use all the laughter I can get.

Your Dearest Darling,

Estrella

46

My Dearest Jim,

I went to Nellie's and had my first bagel in a long time. Don't want to put on the weight I've lost. Happy and Cappy were there. They are thinking of going to Paris for two weeks and can't make up their minds. Paris was beautiful when I saw it 45 years ago. I'm sure it must have changed a lot since then.

Time always wins.

I talk with number one son James every day. He's doing so much better.

I also listened to more of *Greenlights*. Matthew McConaughey bought an airstream and went RV'ing for a while, like I used to try to talk you into doing, but it never happened. You told me that when you passed away I could buy one, but no way! The ones I like are too expensive.

I'm still waiting for that lottery to come through and THEN I will buy me one. Tell G-d to send me that winning ticket!

Your Dearest Darling,

Estrella

47

DEAR JIM,

Today, grief is winning. If people have not gone through it, they simply cannot know. I can barely find the words. And when I do find some, they seem utterly inadequate.

I feel like a thousand elephants have trampled on me. But that's not quite right.

I'm in a black hole and can't see the top. No light filters down. That's not it, either.

My head is in the sand and as soon as I come out it will all be a bad dream that I'm going to wake up from. But it's not.

When I scream, it feels like the top of my head opens up. Like a volcano.

This is what grief feels like, and I don't wish it on anybody.

A big reason I can't get over the grief is because I have such guilt. No one tells you that guilt is grief's neighbor. And since you're not here for me to ask forgiveness, how in G-d's name can I purge this guilt?

Guilt from seeing your eyes looking at me and wondering why I wouldn't feed you or give you water. Hospice told me not to, my darling, on account that you would die painfully. But in your last week, as you hung on, why wouldn't they give you more morphine?

Guilt for not giving you all the morphine I could find.

Guilt for allowing the nurse to talk me into going home. No matter how exhausted I was, I shouldn't have left you in that hospital alone for even a moment.

And because I was home, I have such guilt at not being there to hold your hand when you transitioned into another dimension, if there even is such a thing.

Should I feel guilty for doubting there is?

Grief is not sleeping, wracked with guilt.

Your Dearest Darling,

Estrella

48

My Dearest Jim,

I have the following memories to cling to until the grief finally subsides and I can function in a more normal way.

I will remember...

The day you asked me to marry you in that little bungalow at the end of the street.

The cards you gave me, 42 of them, one to look at each day that I went with Marc to Israel, seven days a week for six weeks, yet because it was such a long flight, I read them all in one go.

The huge, beautiful home you said was ours at Amador Military Base in Panama.

All the delicious meals you prepared for me and I put on 20 pounds!

I will remember...

Dressing up like a princess and going with you to the Officer's Club.

The beautiful Bar Mitzvah you had at our home for my son, Marc.

You taking me to various embassies to represent the Navy diplomatically, walking in holding your arm, both of us dressed to the nines, you so handsome in your Navy Whites and me in beautiful gowns.

And I will remember leaving that fairy tale life in Panama and coming to Florida. I will remember coming to Sarasota and staying with your father for three months while you looked for a job.

I will remember...

Loving you and supporting you while you settled into a civilian life.

Buying our home that we lived in together for 38 years and fixing it up and adding a wonderful lap pool that I use three times a week.

I will remember your patience as a lover.

Your kindness and gentleness.

Your pride in being my husband.

I will remember...

All the beautiful things you made from wood: the desk, the massage table, the cabinets here in this room where I write to you every day.

All your wonderful, exciting "sea stories."

I will remember the kindness you showed my Mother when she came to live with us after my brother passed away.

I will remember so much, my darling, but more than anything I will remember this... the respect, kindness, and love you gave to me.

Thank you for giving me a life filled with beautiful moments that now are cherished memories.

Your Dearest Darling,

Estrella

49

My Dearest Jim,

I called number one son James this morning. It's his 65th birthday. We spoke for almost half an hour. He was in high spirits and we had a good time talking and laughing and even crying a little, too. His doctors say he is doing well. He is as sweet as you are, and we have gotten very close.

I guess you are still around. Through him.

Your Dearest Darling,

Estrella

50

My Darling Jim,

It's 10:30 a.m. and I'm still in pajamas. I just got off the phone with Harry, our friend and handyman. Poor guy. He's been passing kidney stones and WOW was he ever descriptive!

The other day I found chips of paint on the floor and called our advisor at USAA. He came over to see what was happening. There was no damage or leakage found on the roof, but I will have to have the ceiling re-done one of these days. I am so blessed with these people you set up to take care of me. Like my personal team of guardian angels.

I sewed the hem of my pants that finally fit me again! I want to take them on my trip, which is in less than a month. I will miss our home, but it will be good to see everyone and learn more about this retirement community.

I honestly cannot imagine moving, but there are moments when I can't imagine living here a moment longer knowing that you'll never be coming in the door.

Your Dearest Darling,

Estrella

51

My Darling Jim,

I forgot to write yesterday and I feel really sad that I didn't, even though I know these letters are more for me than for you. Does forgetting to write maybe mean that I'm healing?

I checked the pool, and it's a little too cold to go in, so I'll wait until later and get in my exercise.

The gang is waiting for me at Nellie's. I'll write some more later.

I'm back! I spent an hour and a half at Nellie's and laughed a lot with the gang. Cappy had a pain in his neck and I did a little Reiki on him, also the exercise where I ask, "Where is it? What color is it? What shape is it?" I learned this when I did the Erhardt Seminar Training back in 1975. The forum leader asked for a volunteer who had a headache and I raised my hand. In front of almost 500 people—including Lily Tomlin who was in the course with me!—I sat in a director's chair. He had me close my eyes. We did that exercise, and within five minutes the headache was gone.

If only other pains were so clearly and precisely cleansed.

Your Dearest Darling,

Estrella

52

Darling Jim,

I just came back from Temple. I had never been to a Selichot service, and it was very moving. I went so I could have a couple hours of not feeling totally alone. I know you are in a place without suffering and I am glad for you, but I still miss your love, your touch, your voice, YOU, YOU, YOU.

l spoke to number one son James. They have moved him to another rehab place that is in Pomona, and still on the way back from Palm Springs on Highway 10, so I'll be able to see him on my trip before I come back to Sarasota. I won't be able to call him every day since it's a much larger facility, so we decided every two or three days.

Before I left, I turned on the TV and quite by accident started watching a series called *El Rey*. It's in Spanish and about the life of the great mariachi singer Vicente Fernandez. He has a wonderful voice, like some of the old ones like Pedro Infante and Jorge Negrete. Remember how we'd go to the Mexican restaurant and enjoy the mariachis there? You were so generous and always gave them a good tip. I am going to watch more of the series, just to listen to him sing. I'll turn it up nice and loud, so you can listen too.

Your Dearest Darling,

Estrella

53

My Dearest Jim,

Sundays are pretty dreary. I try to do paperwork, since nobody calls and I am not interrupted, but the interruptions help distract me from the emptiness of the house. So much... space. It's been almost three months, and I don't know how to fill that space. And I don't know if I want to. What would even fit?

Staying busy keeps me from pondering such impossible thoughts.

I am washing clothes and hanging them up after they dry, so they don't get wrinkled.

I put out my outfit for Yom Kippur, which is white and represents purity and new beginnings. I feel strangely guilty about having new beginnings, but that's the way G-d designed this, so I will try my best.

I went in for a swim and did my ten laps and got some sun. I'm trying to keep my tan for my trip, so I go out there for about ten minutes every other day.

I watched some more of that series about Vicente Fernandez, *El Rey*. I have to smile when I see the "ez" at the end of many Mexican names, because the "ez" stands for "eretz israel," and that was the ending of names for Jews in Spain during the Spanish Inquisition so that they would not forget their Jewish (Sephardic) roots.

Oh—there's the phone!

I just got off the phone with my sister. She told me she's lonely and cries a lot. I told her I do too. She has not had a partner for many, many years. She belongs to a choir and also to a women's group—interruptions, distractions, business, filling space and time—but she misses being with family. I understand that. Naomi is in Southern California and Marc is in Austin, Texas.

Distance and space are not the same.

Your Dearest Darling,

Estrella

54

Dearest Jim,

I know I haven't written much recently. I've been taking care of business, primarily paperwork, and making necessary phone calls. Who knew our lives could be reduced to such a litany of signatures and waiting on hold?

I didn't even have time today to go to Nellie's. But I swam my laps and worked around the house. I also looked through my medications to make sure I have what I need for my trip.

And I'll admit I really got stuck watching that mariachi series *El Rey*. It brings back my childhood memories of Mexico. Would you believe it's been 21 years since I went there? Most of my cousins have passed on. I think I only have five left and all my aunts and uncles have been gone for a long time.

You should look for them and ask them about me, but nothing embarrassing!

Your Dearest Darling,

Estrella

55

My Dearest Jim,

This morning the Rabbi came over to help me with this little thing called "guilt." You may have heard me mention it from time to time. Yes, that was an attempt at a joke. Not a very good one. But at least I'm trying to face it and laugh at it instead of just giving in to it!

Anyhow, you know Rosh Hashana and Yom Kippur are coming up. So I told her the story about taking you to the doctor who took you off the dementia medicine, and she told me, as others have, that this is not actually guilt. It's GRIEF, and boy am I in it. She reminded me I was a good wife and spent many hours with you in your illness and that I did everything I could to make you comfortable and show you my love. I can't just flip a switch, but I can daily remind myself that grief loves to lie, and I can see through those lies to the truth.

I called number one son James, but it is very difficult to call him at this new facility. I called about five times and couldn't reach him, so they are giving him the message to call me.

Alright my darling, I will take a break and write some more later.

Now I know what it's like to be hooked on a *telenovela*! This *El Rey* has got me so hooked that I won't stop watching until all the episodes are over. The last episode was about the love and soul connection between Vicente Fernandez and his bride Cuca. They were married, and the ceremony was in Spanish, which took me right back to our wedding in Panama, performed by the Justice of the Peace in Spanish and which I believe you understood better than I. I don't even remember the words. All I remember is your eyes on mine, the feeling of the ring sliding onto my finger, the unbelievable warmth and joy that flooded me as we kissed for the first time as husband and wife. Soulmates.

Alright my darling, it's 9pm and I'm going to finish this *El Rey* episode and go to bed. Well, maybe I'll watch another one. Don't tell on me.

Your Dearest Darling,

Estrella

56

My Dearest Jim,

Today I went to Nellie's, and the gang decided that tomorrow we'll wear hats, just to be funny.

Then I went to see Shirley, my grief counselor, for an hour and shared my week with her. I told her about number one son James saying that he would call me instead of me calling him, because it's easier that way.

There's a tropical depression headed our way. We will be safe, but I did two things that you always had us do: I went shopping (water and toilet paper!) and then I filled up the gas tank.

I'll let you know how the hat business goes!

Your Dearest Darling,

Estrella

57

Dear Jim,

This morning at Nellie's, our hat game entertained everyone. Cappy, Happy, and Charlie wore caps, but I pulled out a sexy summer hat and they all went "WOW!" You know which one I mean. It's the one that could always distract you from skimming the pool when I wore it just so...

I must say... it feels much better to blush than to cry.

My series called *El Rey* finally finished with a big bang yesterday. The famous mariachi Vicente Fernandez sang at the Azteca bullfighting ring in Mexico City and he packed the stadium. Maybe you can say hello, because he's now in Heaven. He died last year and his kindness and loyalty to his wife reminds me of you.

I want to write a song just for you, darling. I have written about five, only they don't come out so great in English, so I write them in

Spanish first, then translate them. Happy said she would help me put them on music sheets since she's a pianist.

My trip to Texas and California is in two weeks. Still lots to do before I leave. But I really want to finish your song. So I'm going to work on that now.

Your Dearest Darling,

Estrella

58

My Jim,

Here's your song. Happy will help me with a melody later. But I wanted you to hear it right away.

Your Dearest Darling,

Estrella

My very Dearest Darling

I sit here in our home

It's oh so very quiet

and I hate to be alone

There are many, many others

who sit and cry alone

who try to be the strong ones

in each and every home

We miss our darling partners

our lovers and our friends

My very Dearest Darling

why did you leave me so alone?

Sometimes when it is quiet

I close my eyes and weep

I long to feel your arms around me

and a sweet kiss on the cheek

For some it's merely weeks

For others maybe years

We've loved our darling partners

We've wept so many tears

My very Dearest Darling

I know that you've gone home

But I wish that you could come to me

and never be alone.

59

DEAR SWEET JIM,

Today was quite busy. I swam my laps. I showered and washed my hair. I went to have coffee at Nellie's. When I came home, I did a little work around here, took a nap, and got ready to go to Temple and help put bowls together with dates, apples, honey, sesame candy, and pumpkin seeds. All symbols for Rosh Hashanah.

I was honored to light the candles and usher in the New Year and say the prayer in Hebrew and English. Midway through the English, my tears started flowing. It's my first New Year without you and I miss you so very much.

Shana Tova. Happy New Year. And G-d bless you.

Your Dearest Darling,

Estrella

60

My Dearest Jim,

The news today is that there is a hurricane warning from Tampa to Naples. This one is called Ian. I have done what I could to get ready and I so wish you were here to help me and to feel safe.

I've gotten phone calls from my sister and number one son James. They wanted to make sure I was prepared.

I went to Temple today for the second day of Rosh Hashanah and it was nice, I guess. I read something recently about mourning that said the first year is hardest because everything you go through is the first time without your loved one. First birthday. First anniversary. First new year. And that first-ness amplifies the loss, because all the rituals and traditions are blown up. It's a comforting thought, to think that next year's new year will be easier. But right now, nothing that I go through makes any sense. None of the markers in the calendar. Everything feels wrong and incomplete.

I will NOT celebrate the anniversary of your death. But I will celebrate every birthday and wedding anniversary, my love. The other holidays? I guess we will see what new traditions arise. I can't imagine what they may be.

Your Dearest Darling,

Estrella

61

My Dearest Jim,

It's been a crazy week. I'm sorry I wasn't able to write, but Hurricane Ian made a mess of things, especially south of us. Those poor people. We took some damage on our block. Trees fell on a few homes and several had windows shattered, but thank G-d our home came through whole, except for not having electricity for a week.

I did very well with some help from the neighbors, primarily Mitch and Daniel, who kept my phone charged all the time, so I could respond to those who called to see how I was. I had a couple of offers to stay in their homes, but I feel safe, surrounded by your love with all the beautiful things you made.

I went to Yom Kippur services last night and practically the entire day today. After the services were over and the shofar was sounded, there was a breakfast. Of course, we had bagels, cream cheese, lox, egg salad, tuna salad, and I think that's about all. I can't go to bed yet, I'm too full.

My trip is coming up soon, a week from today. It's bittersweet to go without you, but seeing my family will be nice and I hope to see number one son James as well!

Part of my trip will be on Amtrak, and I will be on the train wishing you were with me, since we both wanted to take a train ride and never got to do it. The one we wanted to do was in the Canadian Rockies, but something always stopped us from doing it. You know, I can't remember what stopped us. What was so much more important than taking that trip together? We truly do not realize our time is limited. We don't know how much time we even have. If we did, would we spend it differently?

Our 41st Anniversary will happen during this trip, so I'll celebrate with my daughters. I'm sure I will cry a lot, but like I told you, I will always celebrate our happy special days.

Your Dearest Darling,

Estrella

62

My Darling Jim,

Today I cleaned out the whole refrigerator and freezer. Everything spoiled with the electricity out for a week.

I also went to the dermatologist today. The rashes and itching I've had for almost six months are much better. They were caused by the stress of your last days and passing, so it wasn't shingles, thank G-d, and I am almost healed.

I had coffee at Nellie's this morning, and Charlie joined me for a few minutes. Then that Navy man we met a few years ago asked to sit with me for a bit. He is a widower, but I'm not interested. There will be no one but you, sweetheart. Ever! I suppose I can have some male friends, but no hanky panky! No sir! You were the only one who could touch me intimately. I am now celibate, and that is fine. I know that isn't always the case for other widows or widowers, but I can't imagine wanting to kiss or touch anyone else.

You better keep your lips and hands to yourself up there, too, mister!

Your Dearest Darling,

Estrella

63

My Darling Jim,

I have been getting ready for this trip, and part of me doesn't want to go. I'm scared to leave this safe space we built together, and to be away from the furniture you built, and the candles that come on by themselves. I fear that your presence in our home gets less every day, and being away for many days... when I get back, will you still be here, or will the house be cold?

Another part of me, though, is incredibly excited to see everyone and give them all big hugs. I haven't seen most of my family on account of illnesses and Covid for about four years. It's time to be with them, even just for a little while.

Before you got sick, remember I joined AFVC (Armed Forces Vacation Club) and for a small fee I could book a two-bedroom, two-bath suite in Palm Springs for some R&R? It was supposed to be for us, but it's been a long and painful six months, and after having to take care of so much business after you went to Heaven, I need a good rest. When I come back, I'll start cleaning out closets. I haven't had the heart to do that yet.

Your Dearest Darling

Estrella

64

My Jim,

I have been away almost a month and have so much to share with you, but first let me tell you about today. I started to unpack but you know that always takes me at least three days to do, and what's worse I had to get used to the time difference from California to Florida, and on top of THAT we just went from "daylight savings" back to "standard time," which sends my body into turmoil. I got home on Monday and here it is Thursday evening and I'm still not all the way back to normal. I even left my cell phone at the Cheesecake Factory and had to go back to get it, which meant driving at night, but I know you were up there taking care of me. It gets harder and harder to drive at night, but I did it!

The trip, honestly, was wonderful. But it's clear it was merely a temporary fix. This house... oh my love. It's just so lonely. If I don't change my life entirely, I'm not sure what I may do.

Let me tell you a little about my trip. I flew directly to San Antonio to meet with Ilene, the gracious lady I have been in contact with for over ten years, regarding Blue Skies of Texas, the retirement community that I so wanted us to see. Well, it is lovely. Beyond what I was expecting. I stayed in a beautiful guest bedroom, but before going to bed, I went to the dining room where they were just finishing up the monthly birthday celebrations for October. People were dancing to a great band that played music from the 50s to the 80s. I was tempted to join in the dancing.

The next morning Ilene showed me around to different apartments and they were so impressive. Newly renovated. Well-maintained. Kitchens bigger than ours (you know how I always disliked our small kitchen even though I love our house).

The third day Ilene was busy, so I went to the on-site bistro for breakfast and met some really welcoming ladies, all widows like me.

The next day, Ilene drove me all the way to Austin to be with Marc and his family. Highlights included a lunch where I had a Mai Tai, but it was so strong I couldn't finish it. I switched to a "Gilligan's Island," much milder, but even so, when we got home, I wasn't feeling too good. I actually threw up! No more Mai Tai's for me!!!

We also went on a "safari" at the zoo. It was surprisingly educational! Do you know why giraffes have long eyelashes? They eat from a tree that has a lot of thorns and the eyelashes protect them from getting stabbed. The tour guy said that if the sap from that tree touches a human being, it could kill us. Imagine that. Eyelashes protecting such a large creature from poisonous sap. Small things matter. More than we know.

And I got to see number one son James! When we got to the rehab center, there was James and the first thing he said to me was, "*Hola senorita, como estas?*" I grabbed him and gave him the biggest hug and kiss. Oh he looks so much like you! We went to an IHOP. I had a waffle, and he ordered a shake, and then he nibbled on my waffle. We talked for an hour and a half. I invited him to come to Sarasota, both to visit and to see what he wanted that belonged to you. I will give him my "sky miles" and told him so.

When we got back to the rehab center, he introduced me to about twenty people, some staff and other residents. That touched my heart. He kept saying, "This is my mother. She came all the way from Florida to see me." The five-minute goodbye turned into twenty. I gave him another hug and said we'll keep each other posted. I brought him your sweatshirt hoody with the Engelhardt crest and name. When he put it on… oh, Jim. Can a heart be full of agony and joy at the same time?

And now I'm home. But is it "home" without you? I don't know that home is a place. Home… is an energy held between people, maybe?

I'm sure you hear in my letters that I'm thinking of moving to Blue Skies in Texas. But I'm just not sure what to do.

Might you give me a sign?

Your Dearest Darling,

Estrella

65

My Beloved Jim,

Today was Thanksgiving and I must have cried seven times missing you, maybe more. Another "first." The first Thanksgiving without you. Thank G-d I'll never have another one of those.

I can't seem to get motivated. I waste a lot of time. I went to a very nice restaurant with some friends. It was expensive and not as delicious as the turkeys you used to make.

You used to say, "Life is a shit sandwich and we all have to take a bite."

Well. I've had my fill.

Your Dearest Darling,

Estrella

66

My Dearest Jim,

I am waiting for a sign from you. Please help me understand what I'm supposed to do next. I fear having guilt if I leave. I fear being turned inside out with grief if I stay.

That damn "guilt" again. I actually wonder if I did something wrong to have you get sick. That G-d is punishing me for something by taking you away. Silly, maybe. And I know that "guilt" is part of the grieving process. I try to understand and accept this. I envy those who can. Believe me, I try.

There is a neighbor two blocks from here. As I was driving by, he waved and I stopped to say hello. He lost his wife thirteen years ago and recently lost his girlfriend, too. I told him to call me if he needed to talk. Then he asked me if I would have dinner with him. I hesitated, but then said OK. It feels really strange. I don't want to go out with any man alone, but I felt sorry for him. He looked like he was about to cry (and I should know!). I actually feel guilty—big surprise—but I know you wouldn't like me to be lonely.

And I still feel married to you.

Your Dearest Darling,

Estrella

67

Darling Jim,

Today I cleaned out four drawers in the beautiful hutches you made. I also cleaned out one cabinet. On Sunday I will finish the other one. There's stuff in there we haven't used in years. Some things I'm donating to Vietnam veterans. They need everything, but clothes more than anything. I'm having a hard time giving up your clothes. Every piece I take out reminds me of a time we were together, so I hug and kiss them to make them loved, and wash them one last time. Washing them removes your scent. It's easier to fold them and box them up when they don't smell like you. And knowing they will warm and protect your fellow veterans gives me peace of mind, even if my heart still has to catch up.

I made a very nice dish of vegetables with mushrooms, garlic, celery, scallions, and zucchini with some brown rice and a sliced banana on the side. It was delicious. I lit my Sabbath candles and put your yarmulka right next to them.

Now I'm watching *Somebody Feed Phil*. I really enjoy the show. I think you would have, too. After all, you were a superb chef.

That one tiny word… *were*. The difference between *are* and *were*…

It's a chasm.

Your Dearest Darling,

Estrella

68

Dear Jim,

Today, I met with a realtor and showed him our home. He's the same fellow who saw our home twenty years ago when we were looking at moving to Tennessee, but it didn't work out and we never moved. Now he looked again and was impressed with how we've improved and maintained our home, so we will see whether this time I do it.

Please understand I only invited him because I'm trying to get all the information and see the pluses and minuses of all my options. It's hard enough to have lost you and now, perhaps, our home? But I have to see what is best for me, since I don't have you to take care of me anymore and I refuse to be a burden to my family.

A sign, please. A sign.

I love Sarasota, but everywhere I turn there are so many memories. I see you everywhere. Maybe that's why I can't help but cry so much.

So would it be better to make a change? I would miss my friends here and miss going to classes and Nellie's and the theatre. Would I be able to make new friends at Blues Skies in Texas?

I had hoped the trip would make things clear. But now, instead of just lost, I also feel confused.

All I know is I love you forever.

Your Dearest Darling,

Estrella

69

My Dearest Jim,

Today is the first night of Hanukkah. I'm going to Temple where everyone is bringing their menorahs and lighting the first candle. How I wish that you could go with me.

I made some potato latkes and ate them myself. They were good, but didn't have quite the spirit of eating with you the ones Craig used to make at Nellie's. I hope he's making a huge batch up there in Heaven for you and everyone!

Christmas is just around the corner. I wrote a card to your sister, one to Ilene at Blue Skies of Texas, and another to number one son James. I need to do a few more. I've been getting lots of cards and even an e-Hanukkah card. People are kind, though it's clear they aren't sure what to say. Again, it's the FIRST. The first Hanukkah and Christmas when it's just me. One Engelhardt, not two. Some people are afraid to mention you. Others try too hard to make it all normal. I don't hold it against any of them.

OK I am running late for Temple, so I must sign off.

I love you.

Your Dearest Darling,

Estrella

70

My Jim,

I just got home from Temple. The service was lovely, but that is not why I am writing to you again today, late at night.

It's the candles.

The candles are not lit.

I checked the switches. They are still on.

So it must be the batteries. They have died.

Is this your sign? Your message to me? Are you truly gone? Are you telling me it's ok for me to leave, too? I don't mean *leave* as in doing something bad, even though that still occasionally crosses my mind. I could never do that.

But to leave our home?

I don't want to replace the batteries, even though I miss the light.

Your Dearest Darling,

Estrella

71

My Very Dearest Jim,

I see the house differently since the candles went out.

I took a few days to think about it.

I will be moving to Blue Skies of Texas, the retirement community I've been talking about so much. Soon.

In Texas I will be cared for and even get healthier from the comaraderie and activities that I can't seem to get into here in Sarasota. My apartment will be lovely and they're even going to repaint it to my chosen color scheme.

It's a two-bedroom, two-bath, so I can have visitors, like number one son James or my kids or even friends visiting from Sarasota. They can stay up to 30 days if they want!

The kitchen is larger than the one in our house, really nice, new appliances, and there's even a butler's pantry and lots of cupboard space.

The swimming pool is Olympic-size and indoors, so I'll be able to swim year round. There is also a theatre group, ukulele and singing group, and many more activities, so I know I'm going to be distracted and stimulated. You know how I enjoy meeting new people, plus I'll be closer to all our family.

There is Independent Living and three other types. Hopefully, I won't need the others and I plan to be there twenty years—I'm 82 going on 62!—so the cowgirl in me is excited to go there.

This is the first time since you left that I've thought about twenty years stretching out before me... and not been terrified or cried. I am trusting you are happy about this. After all, you're in Heaven, so what difference does it make if I'm in Florida or Texas?

The excitement of moving isn't replacing or lessening my grief. But now my grief isn't alone. It's no longer the only voice.

I have so much to do to get ready. I probably won't write as much, or at all, at least until I'm settled in. Then I'm sure I'll have so much to tell you about.

No matter what, I remain—and will always be—

Your Dearest Darling,

Estrella

72

My Dearest Jim,

I just read back through all my letters to you. I know I said I wouldn't write to you again until I was in Texas, since it seems you are no longer here in our house with me. But reading back and re-living the past half-year through these words... I had to tell you what I've realized.

I have read so much about mourning and grief. No one definition could possibly fit everyone's experience. Grief has shades. Mourning is grief in action. Even day by day, as grief ebbs and flows, the action of my mourning course-corrects. It can feel like being dragged by a horse. It can feel like riding a tornado. It can feel like being caught in an avalanche, buried in airless cold.

And for someone else, it could feel completely different.

Someone wrote, "The more you love, the harder you grieve." I agree, but in no way would I advocate for anyone to love any less. Loving less may mean avoiding the deepest trenches of grief. But loving less would also mean your peaks of joy have been shorter, and your moments of bliss briefer. Everything is a tradeoff.

This has helped me understand that the unspeakable depth of my grief is actually a testament to you and our love. It doesn't hurt less. But it hurts differently. In a way I can cope with.

Oh, my love. We were so lucky. To love deeply is a privilege not afforded to all. Yes, it makes my grieving harder, and I would never wish this pain on anyone, but also never would I wish anyone to miss out on the chance to share their life with a soulmate.

They say when you marry you become "one flesh," right? So when you lose a part of yourself, are you condemned to live half a life? I can't believe G-d or you would want that for me. There are moments when it has felt like half a life. But now, looking ahead, I see how I can continue to have a complete and full life, and my doing so in no way diminishes my memories of you or how important you are.

Pain is mandatory. But I'm coming to see that suffering is optional. You used to tell me I like to suffer. You're damn right I do! By suffering, I show you I love you. And when you look out at the world, you see that people who suffer can claim the higher moral ground and a certain "expertise." In a real way, humans cherish their suffering, which only again proves that most suffering is by choice.

I don't want to lose my pain. The pain reminds me of how precious you were. But the suffering... my love, for you I am doing my best to stop choosing to suffer.

You gave me the most beautiful gift: you loved me with kindness, with respect, with gentility. Whether sexually, spiritually, emotionally, or intellectually, you always took care of me and supported me, and yet had the humility to accept that same depth of love from me. I think it is easier to love than to be loved. Most of us, deep down where we don't let others look, don't really think we deserve it. You proved to me I do.

And with that, dear man, I shall sign off, and turn to the future, knowing you are with me. I still may put your picture on the pillow next to me at night, and your letter to me will always be in my wallet, your voice just a few unfoldings away. But you should know...

I'm going to be ok.

I love you, my Jim. With everything I have and everything I am.

Your Dearest Darling,

Estrella

EPILOGUE

My Dearest Darling,

I promise you my love for today and tomorrow.

I promise you as much happiness as I can give.

I promise not to doubt you or mistrust you, but to grow and add to your life of content.

I promise never to try to change you, but I will accept with understanding the changes you make in your life.

Most important, I will accept your love for me without fear of tomorrow, knowing that tomorrow I'll love you so much more than today.

Forever yours—

Jim

ACKNOWLEDGEMENTS

Thank you to Jason Cannon for being my teacher, editor, cheerleader, and publisher.

Thank you also to Alice Brodhead for donating her talent and skill as an artist. Your love for Jim and me is so beautifully apparent in the cover art you painted.

And thank you to all my friends and family, many of whom feature in this book. Without you, I would not have survived the loss of our beloved Jim.

ESTRELLA ENGELHARDT has been a student of life for 82 years. She is mother to two adult children and stepmother to five more.

She has been involved in International Folk Dancing for twenty years and theatre performance for sixteen years. She also became a Massage Therapist at age 55 and a Hair Stylist from the Vidal Sassoon Academy in 1975.

She graduated Panama Canal College with a degree in Physical Education/Psychology, and has traveled extensively throughout Europe, Mexico, Central and South America, Panama, Israel, and Scandinavia.

Letters to Jim is her first book.